Great African Americans

Louis Armstrong

jazz musician

Revised Edition

Patricia and Fredrick McKissack

Series Consultant
Dr. Russell L. Adams, Chairman
Department of Afro-American Studies, Howard University

Enslow Publishers, Inc.

40 Industrial Road	PO Box 38
Box 398	Aldershot
Berkeley Heights, NJ 07922	Hants GU12 6BP
USA	UK

http://www.enslow.com

To Robert Carwell, Sr.
A special thanks to our friends
at the Missouri Historical Society in St. Louis

Copyright © 2001 by Enslow Publishers, Inc.

Revised edition of Louis Armstrong: Jazz Musician © 1991

Library of Congress Cataloging-in-Publication Data

McKissack, Pat, 1944-
    Louis Armstrong : jazz musician / Patricia and Fredrick McKissack.—Rev. ed.
        p. cm. – (Great African Americans)
   Includes bibliographical references (p.   ) and index.
   ISBN 0-7660-1675-7
    1. Armstrong, Louis, 1901—1971—Juvenile literature. 2. Jazz musicians—United
States—Biography—Juvenile literature. [1. Armstrong, Louis, 1901—1971. 2. Musicians.
3. Jazz. 4. African Americans—Biography.] I. McKissack, Fredrick. II. Title.
   ML3930.A75 M4 2001
   781.65'092—dc21

                00-012426

Printed in the United States of America

10 9 8 7 6 5

To Our Readers
We have done our best to make sure all Internet addresses in this book were active and appropriate when we went to press. However, the author and the publisher have no control over and assume no liability for the material available on those Internet sites or on other Web sites they may link to. Any comments or suggestions can be sent by e-mail to comments@enslow.com or to the address on the back cover.

Every effort has been made to locate all copyright holders of material used in this book. If any errors or omissions have occurred, corrections will be made in future editions of this book.

Illustration Credits: Block Brothers Studio, Missouri Historical Society, St. Louis, p. 7; Courtesy of the Hogan Jazz Archives, Tulane University, p. 10; Courtesy of the Hogan Jazz Archives, Tulane University; Ralston Crowford, photographer, p. 6; Library of Congress, pp. 3, 4, 18, 22 (#3, #4), 25; Louis Armstrong House & Archives at Queens College/CUNY, pp. 8, 11, 22 (#1, #2), 26, 27; Moorland-Spingarn Research Center, Howard University, pp. 17, 21, 24; National Archives, pp. 14–15, 16; Pierce W. Hangge, Missouri Historical Society, St. Louis, p. 12.

Cover Credits: Library of Congress; Louis Armstrong House & Archives at Queens College/CUNY; Moorland-Spingarn Research Center, Howard University; National Archives.

TaBLe of CONTENTS

Louis Armstrong
August 4, 1901–July 6, 1971

CHAPTER 1

Off to a Bad Start

i n 1900, New Orleans, Louisiana, was a busy city. One of the places people liked to go for a good time was Black Storyville.

Black Storyville had lots of bars and dance halls. There were lots of fights. Louis Armstrong was born in Storyville on August 4, 1901.

Louis's family was very poor. His mother, Mayann, did different jobs. Grandmama Josephine took care of Louis until he was five years old.

Grandmama Josephine lived in one of these row homes in New Orleans. She took care of Louis until he was about five years old.

Then he went to live with his mother and his little sister, who was called Mama Lucy. Their home was a one-room shack. Louis's father was not around very much.

Black Storyville was full of crime. But something very special was happening there. A new kind of music was being played. It was called jazz.

6

Louis loved the sound of Storyville jazz. It was a part of him. No other music was like jazz. It was special.

Grandmama Josephine took Louis to church almost every Sunday. Louis enjoyed singing the old spirituals. Those old songs were special to him, too.

Dixieland Jazz was a new and exciting kind of music. The Cotton Club Band from St. Louis was a famous band of the time.

7

Louis often skipped school. Instead he sold newspapers on the street. He used the money to help buy food for his family. He dropped out of school when he was eleven.

"You're going to end up in trouble," Grandmama Josephine always warned Louis. And she was right.

Louis and his sister, Beatrice, posed for a picture with their mother, Mayann.

8

CHAPTER 2

In Trouble

Louis and three of his friends started a singing group. They sang on street corners for money.

One day Louis found a gun in an old trunk. He waited until New Year's Eve. He wanted to greet the New Year with loud gunshots. On the street, a boy fired a small gun. Then Louis shot his gun. His friends laughed and cheered. He pointed the gun into the air . . . and pulled the trigger.

Suddenly a policeman took hold of Louis.

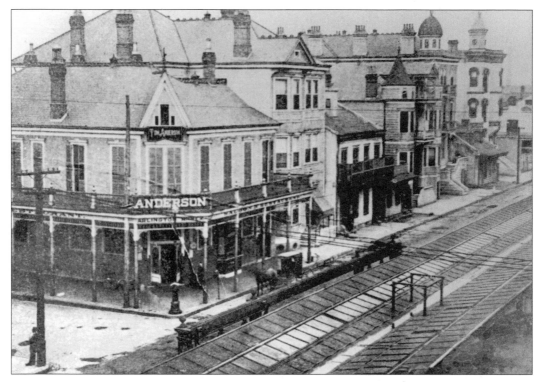

Storyville in New Orleans in the early 1900s.

The bullets were not real. No one was really hurt. Louis was just trying to have fun.

But the judge didn't see it that way. Louis broke the law. He was sent to reform school.

Louis was twelve years old. "I thought the world was coming to an end," he said later.

Peter Davis taught music at the school.

Louis was sent to reform school at the Colored Waifs' Home for Boys, left. There he joined the brass band.

He asked Louis to play the cornet. Louis joined the brass band. By the end of the year, he was leading the band.

People loved jazz. It was happy music. It was played on riverboats that took people down the Mississippi River to New Orleans.

Once Louis led the band through Storyville. His family cheered. So did his friends. It was a day Louis never forgot.

Louis stayed in reform school for about two years. "Being there saved my life," he said years later.

CHAPTER 3

And All That Jazz

Louis was sent to live with his father. But before long, he was back with his mother in Black Storyville.

He took a job driving a cart full of coal. With his money, he bought an old horn. He started playing with jazz bands in Storyville bars. He worked all day and played his horn at night.

In 1917 many black jazz musicians went to Chicago and New York to play. One great trumpeter was Joe Oliver. He liked Louis. Louis thought Oliver was the best trumpeter.

When Oliver left for Chicago, Louis was asked to take his seat in the Kid Ory Band. At last Louis got a chance to be heard.

Soon people were coming to Black Storyville just to hear Louis Armstrong.

Joe Oliver asked Louis to come play the cornet in Chicago. So he went. There he married Lil Hardin. She played the piano.

'Lil wanted Louis to start his own band. But Louis wasn't ready. He played with some of the best bands in New York and Chicago.

Louis worked on a riverboat during the summer of 1919. He washed dishes and also played in the band (third from right).

The King Oliver Band, with King Oliver, seated; Lil Hardin, right; and Louis Armstrong, third from right.

In the 1920s, everyone was talking about jazz . . . jazz . . . and more jazz. And the jazz player most people were talking about was Louis Armstrong.

In 1929, Louis was in *Hot Chocolates*, a Broadway musical.
He also made several hit records.

Jazz is a
"hot sound,"
said Louis.

CHAPTER 4

Oh, Yeaaaaah!

For many years Louis played the cornet. One night he played the trumpet. It was larger than the cornet. He liked its sound. From then on he played the trumpet.

Louis also made records with many different bands. More and more people heard his music. He made them love the sounds of Storyville jazz the same way he did. "It's a hot sound," he said. Then he would wipe his face with a big, white handkerchief.

Cornet

Violin

Alto
Saxophone

Trumpet

Slide Trombone

Double
Bass

Clarinet

Grand
Piano

At last Louis started his own band. They went all over the United States playing jazz . . . jazz . . . and more jazz.

Sometimes when Louis played he also sang. His voice sounded like he had a bad cold. But that was his own special sound.

"Music makes me happy," said Louis. "I want to make you happy, too." And he did.

There is a story people tell about Louis Armstrong. It may or may not be true. It is said that one night he was singing and forgot the words. So he made trumpet sounds with his voice. Do-skid-dat-de-dat-dat-do. That way of singing is called scatting.

And at the end of a song, Louis always sang, "Oh, yeaaaaah!" People waited so that they could join him in singing, "Oh, yeaaaaah!"

Louis Armstrong House & Archives at Queens College/CUNY (1 & 2)

Louis played his music all over the world: 1. In Japan in 1954.
2. In Egypt with his wife, Lucille, in 1961. 3. In Africa in 1956.
4. People of all ages and interests loved his music. This fan asked
for an autograph on his head!

c h a p t e r   5

Satchmo

L ouis had not taken his band to New Orleans. So in 1931 he went back to his home city.

His mother, Mayann, had died in 1927. But the rest of his family came to hear his band play.

Some people in the South thought black and white musicians should not play together in the same band. Louis thought differently. His band had members of different races. So Louis and his band were turned away from some hotels.

They were called names. But his band stayed together and played great music. Lots of people came to hear them, and they enjoyed the music.

Louis's friends called him "Satchel Mouth" because his smile was so big. (A satchel is a suitcase that opens wide.) Over the years, "Satchel Mouth" became "Satchmo." By the late 1930s, everybody was calling Louis "Satchmo." And he loved it.

Satchmo won many awards.

Louis and Lil were no longer together. There were always large crowds around him. But Satchmo was lonely. His music was sad. Then he married Lucille Wilson, a beautiful dancer. Satchmo was happy again. So was his music.

In 1960, Louis Armstrong was named a goodwill ambassador. He went all over the world playing music and making friends.

Louis with actress Grace Kelly in a publicity photo for the 1950 movie *High Society*.

Louis was
one of
the most
popular
jazz artists
in history.

Louis Armstrong House & Archives at Queens College/CUNY (pg. 26 & top pg. 27)

Satchmo made many records. He was in several movies. He had one big hit song: *"Hello, Dolly!"* It sold millions of copies. He also won many awards. He never wanted to stop playing music.

And he never did. He lived and made music until he was almost seventy years old.

He died on July 6, 1971.

Louis enjoyed blowing his horn with neighborhood children in Queens, New York.

timeLINe

1922

1901 ~ Louis Armstrong is born on August 4 in New Orleans, Louisiana.

1912 ~ Is sent to reform school.

1913 ~ Begins a professional career as a cornet player.

1917 ~ Replaces Joe Oliver in the Kid Ory Band.

1922 ~ Joins Oliver's Creole Jazz Band in Chicago.

1927 ~ Louis's mother, Mayann, dies in Chicago.

1929 ~ Stars in *Hot Chocolates*, a Broadway musical.

1931 ~ Returns to New Orleans, Louisiana, to perform.

1929

1932 ~ Begins first European tour.

1936 ~ First autobiography is published: *Swing That Music*.

1943 ~ Moves to Corona, Queens, New York City.

1964 ~ "Hello, Dolly!" becomes a number-one hit song.

1971 ~ Dies on July 6.

WORDS TO KNOW

award—An honor given to a person who has done something special.

brass band—A group of musicians who play the brass horns: trombone, tuba, French horn, trumpet, or cornet.

cornet—A brass horn; a musical instrument.

dance hall—A place where people go to dance.

goodwill ambassador—A person who represents the United States around the world.

handkerchief—square piece of cloth used by people to wipe their face, hands, or noses.

jazz—A special type of music developed in the early 1900s.

judge—The person who decides a court case.

musicians—People who play instruments and make music.

reform school—A special school where children who get into trouble with the law are sent.

29

WORDS TO KNOW

"Satchel Mouth"—A playful name given to Louis Armstrong because of his very large mouth. A satchel is a kind of suitcase that opens wide.

scatting—A kind of singing without using words. A person's voice is used to make sounds like an instrument.

spirituals—Religious songs that were first sung by African-American slaves.

trumpet—A brass horn; a musical instrument.

trumpeter—A person who plays the trumpet.

Learn more about Louis Armstrong

Books

Monceaux, Morgan. *Jazz: My Music, My People*. New York: Knopf, 1994.

Old, Wendie, *Louis Armstrong: King of Jazz*. Enslow Publishers, Inc., 1998.

Orgill, Roxanne, *If I Only Had a Horn: Young Louis Armstrong*. Houghton Mifflin Co., 1997.

Music

Ken Burns Jazz Collection: Louis Armstrong. Sony/Columbia, 2000.

Internet Addresses

Louis Armstrong: A Cultural Legacy
<http://www.npg.si.edu/exh/armstrong/index.htm>

Jazz Kids: Now and Then
<http://www.pbs.org/jazz/kids/nowthen/louis.html>

Louis Armstrong Discography
<http://www.satchography.com>

index